Curious Creatures

FUN-SCHOOLING

NOTEBOOK

color ~ doodle ~ learn ~ write

Sarah Janisse Brown

MY FUN-SCHOOLING
NOTEBOOK

NAME:_____

DATE:_____

How to use this book:

1. There are no real instructions.
2. This is your book. Enjoy it!
3. Write and draw anything you like.
4. If you want to color, doodle or take notes, you can. Just have fun!

Illustrations by Sarah Janisse Brown
With advice from
Susannah Autumn Brown - age 10
The Thinking Tree, LLC
FunSchoolingBooks.com

Coloring
Time

Nature Study

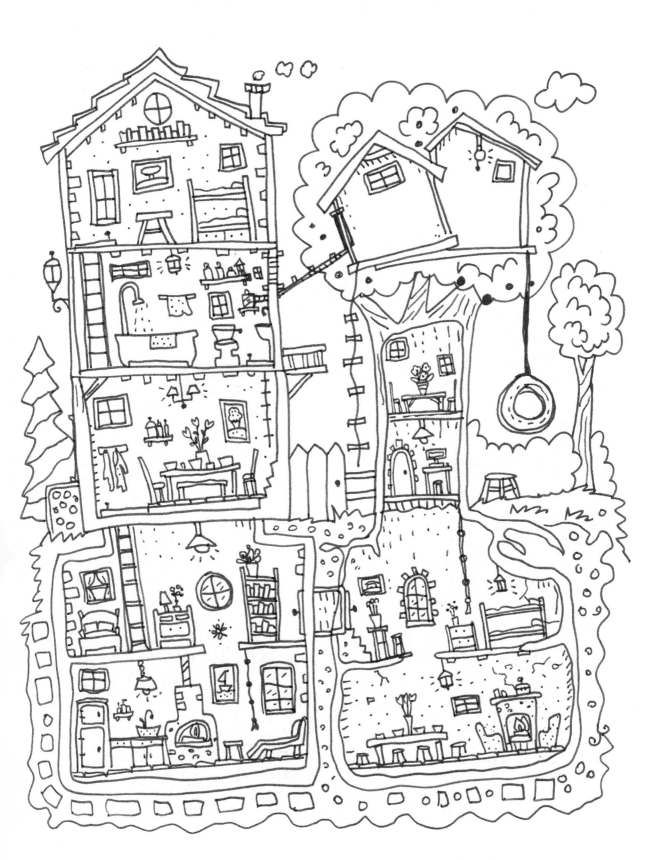

_____

_____

_____

_____

_____

_____

_____

_____

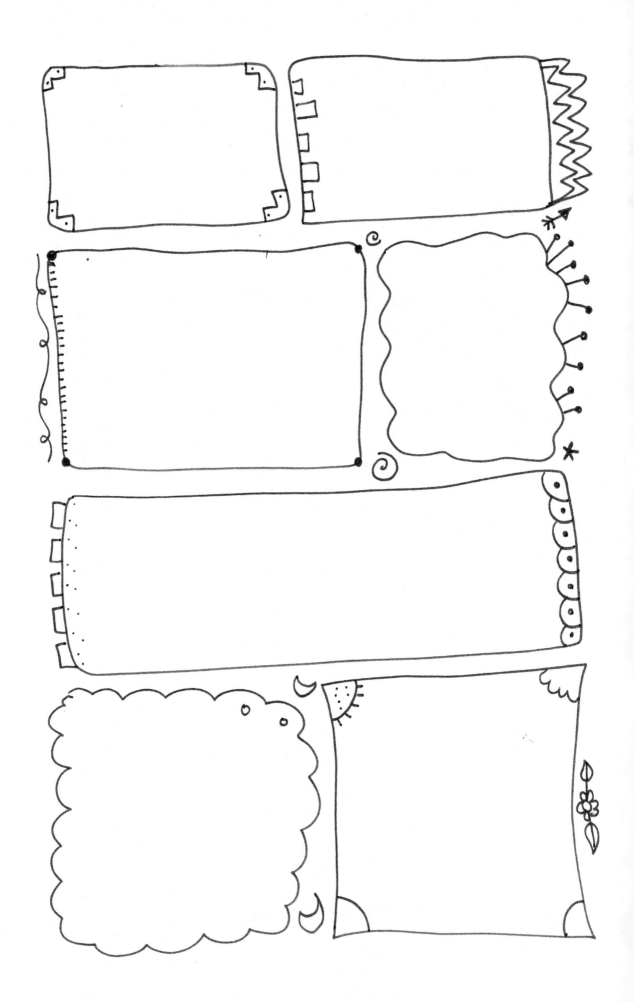

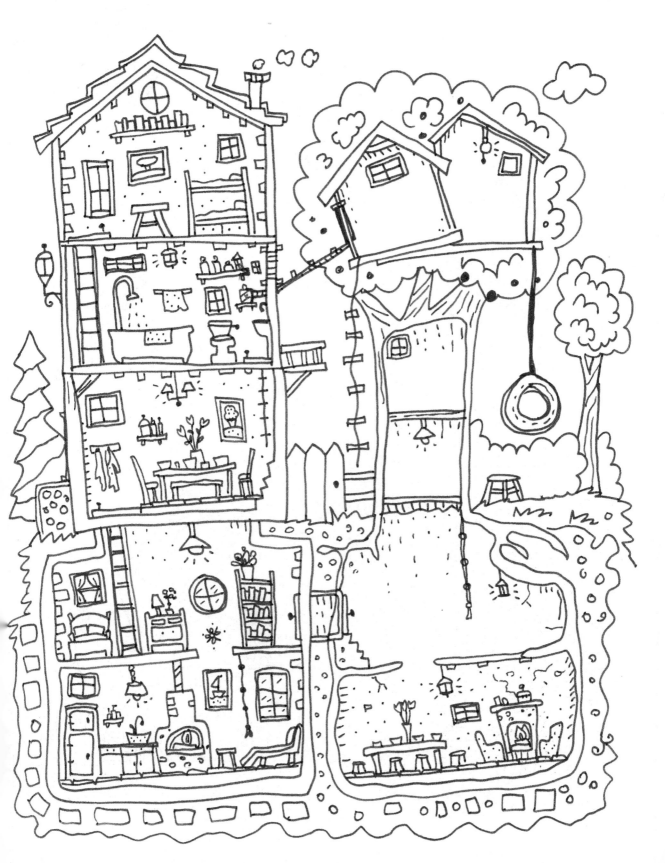

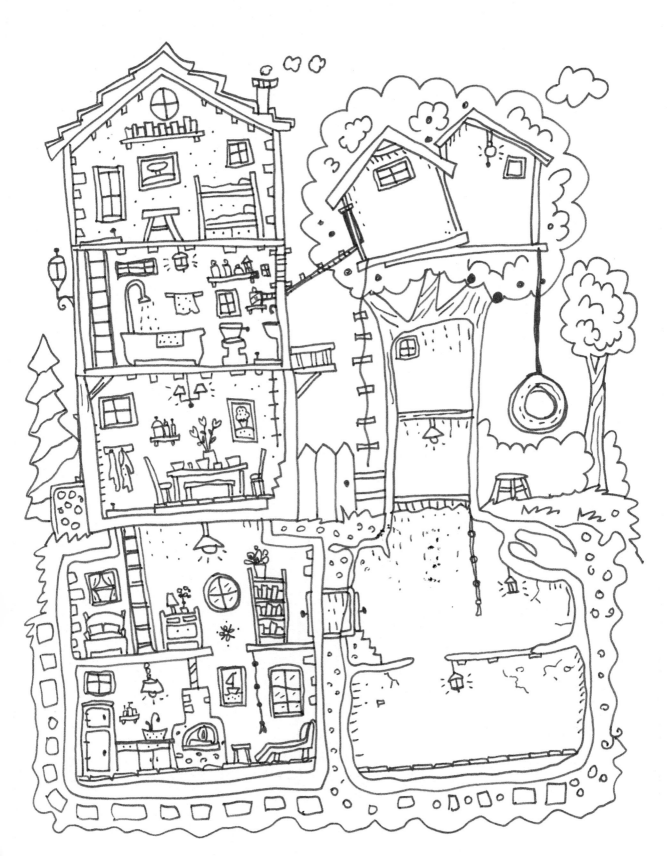

⟳	1.	2.	3.	4.

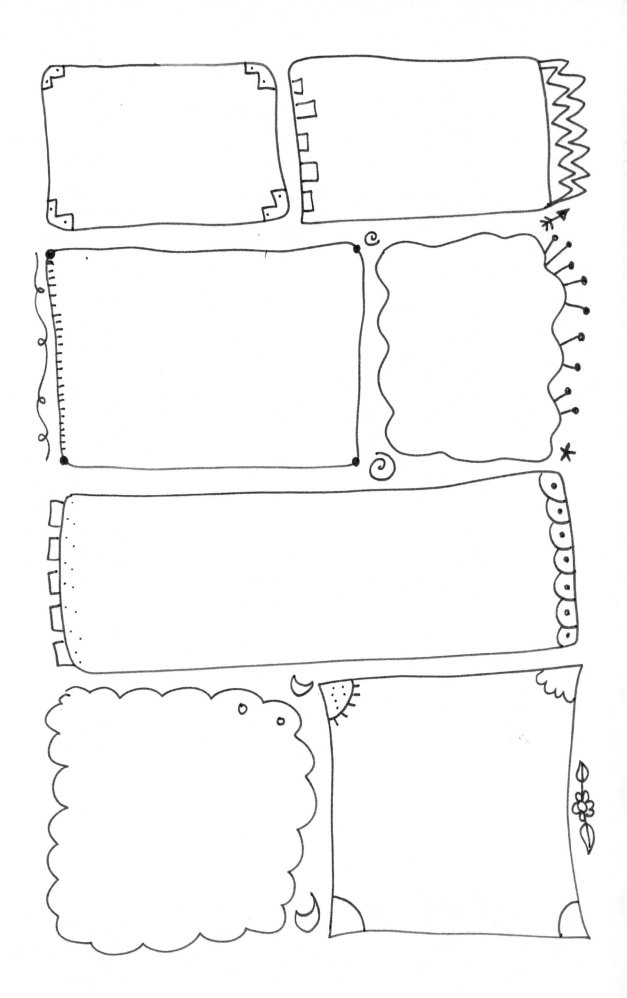

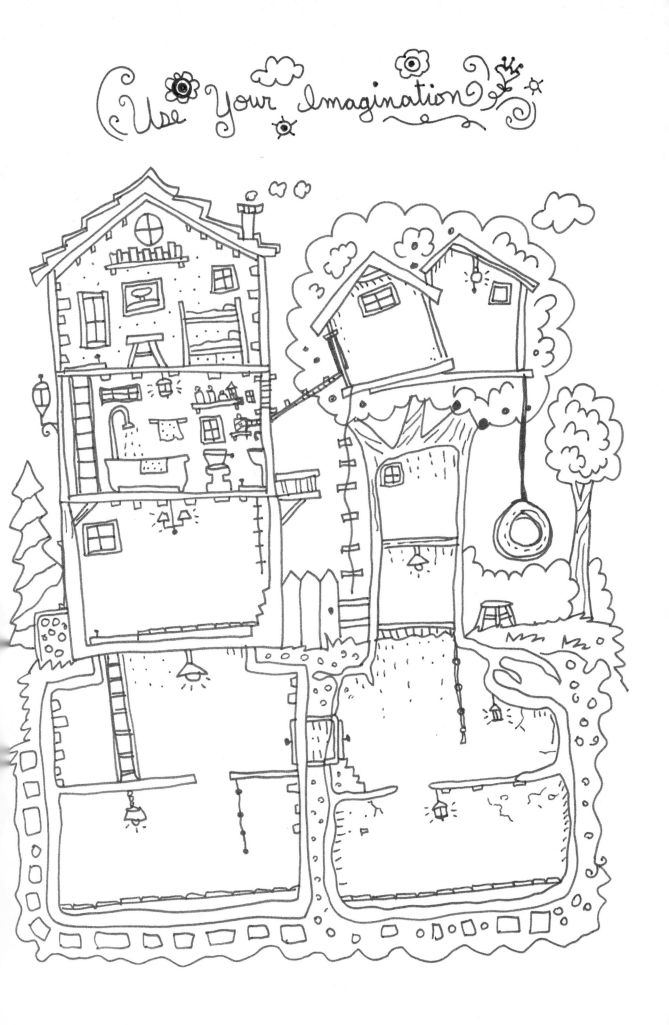

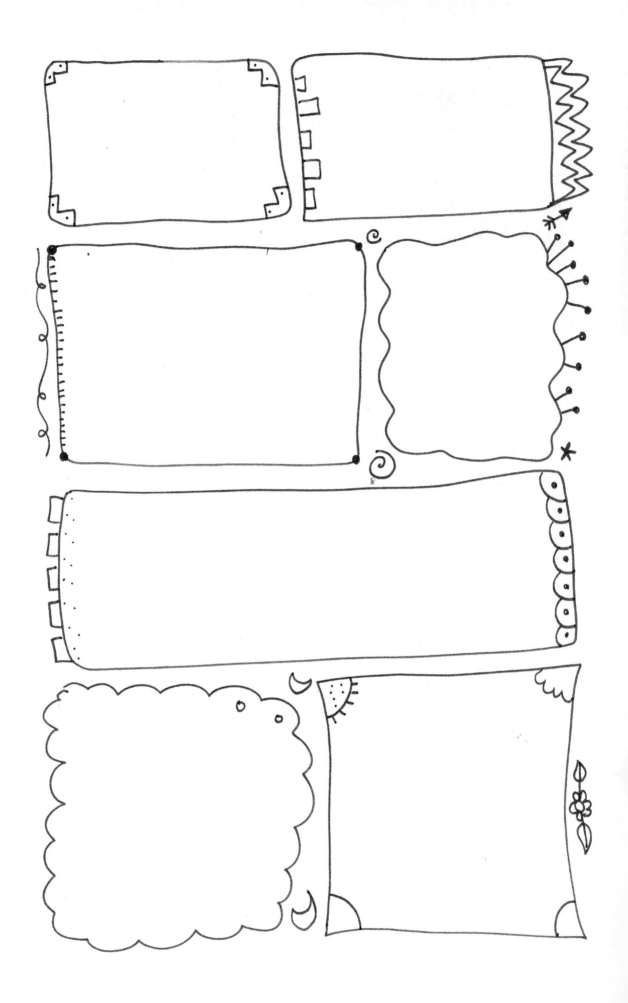

Use Your Imagination

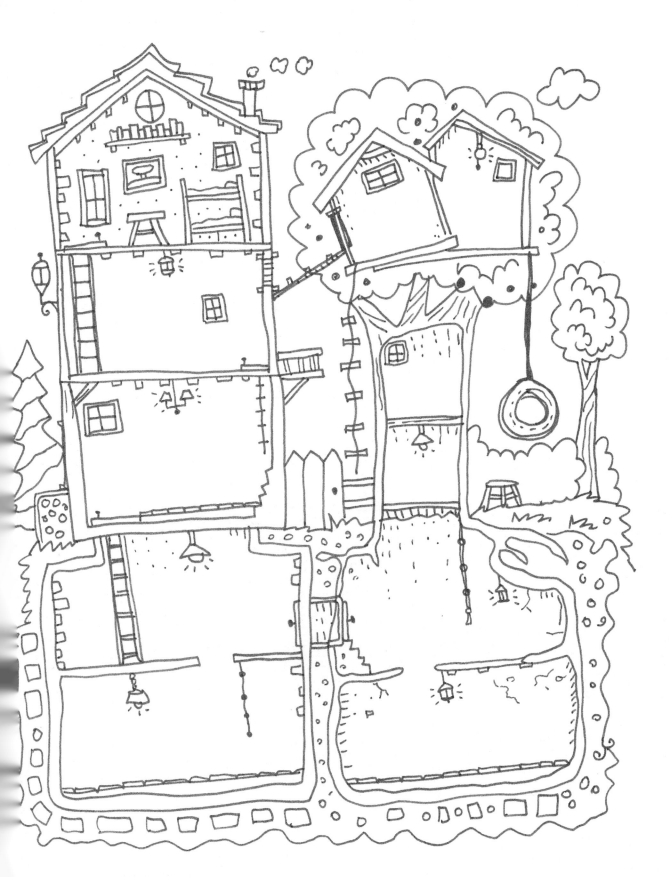

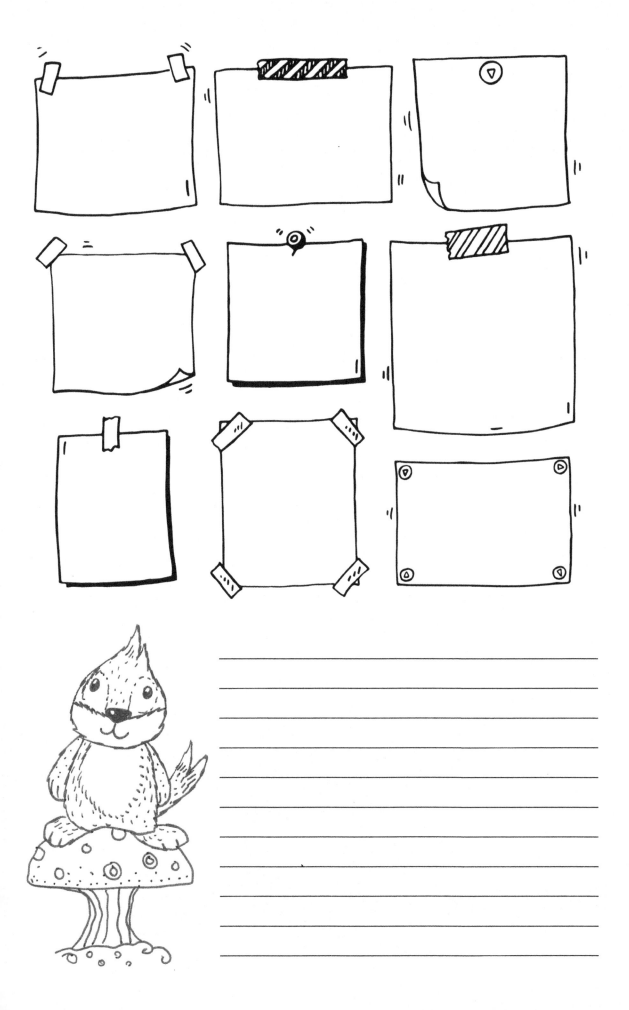

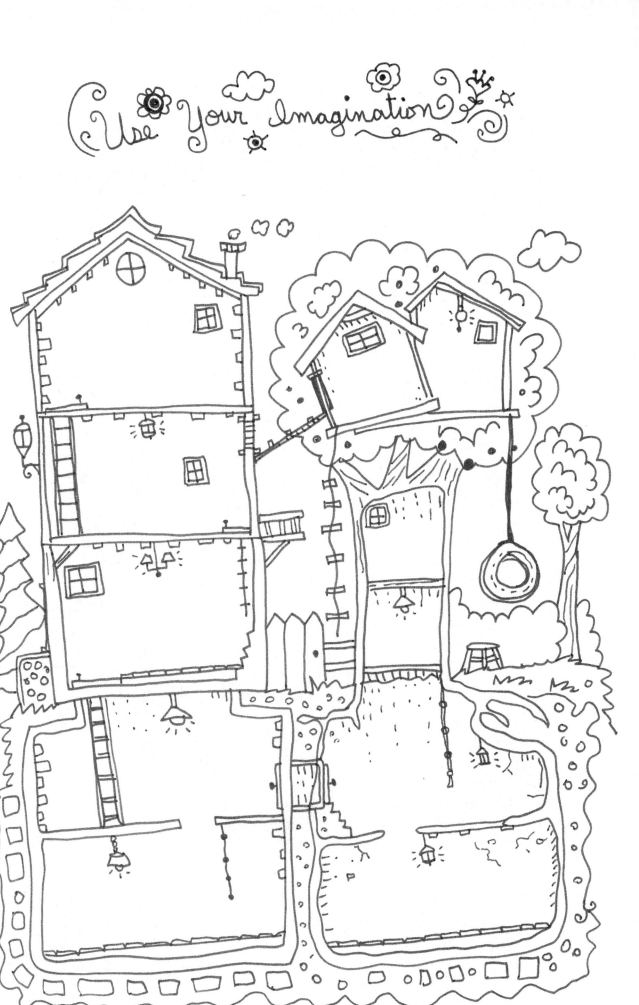

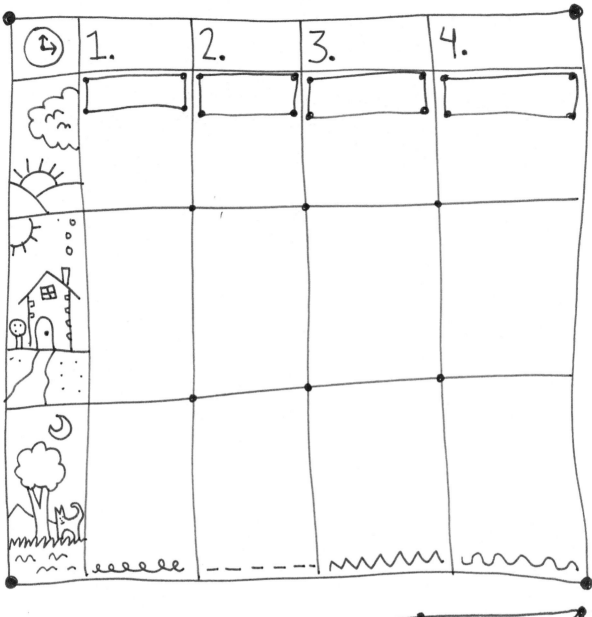

↻	1.	2.	3.	4.

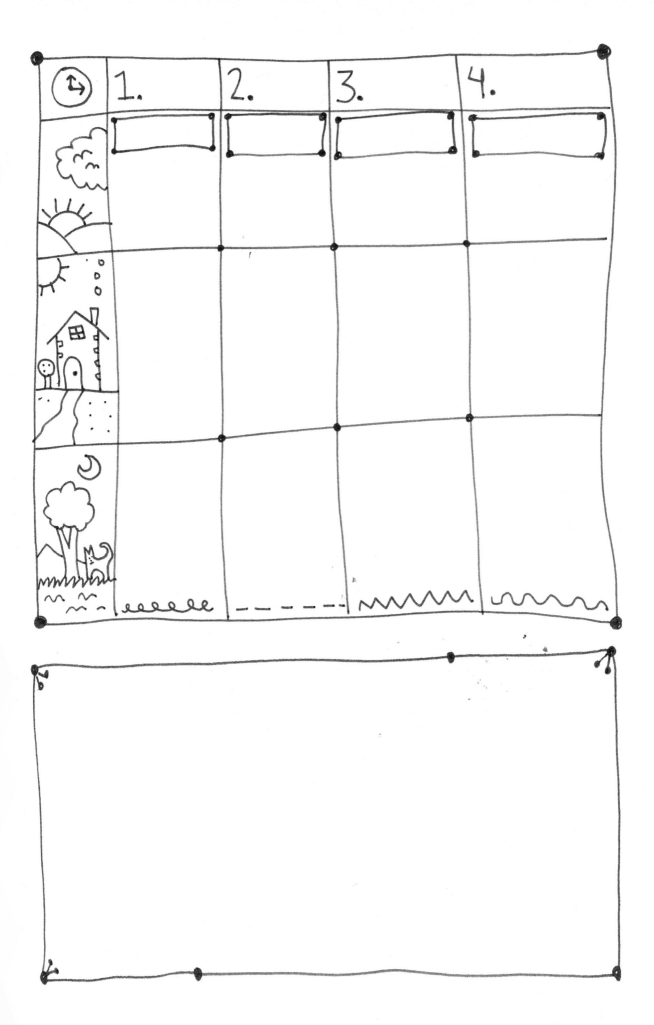

Notes * Anything * Ideas

Memories

Plans

Doodles

Thoughts

Letters

Numbers
1 2 3

Dreams   Research   Drawings

Notes * Anything * Ideas

Memories

Plans

Doodles

Thoughts

Letters

Numbers
1 2 3

Dreams Research Drawings

Notes * Anything * Ideas

Memories

Plans

Doodles

Thoughts

Letters

Numbers
1 2 3

Dreams   Research   Drawings

Notes * Anything * Ideas

Memories

Plans

Doodles

Thoughts

Letters

Numbers
1 2 3

Dreams   Research   Drawings

Notes   * Anything *   Ideas

Memories

Plans

Doodles

Thoughts

Letters

Numbers
1 2 3

Dreams   Research   Drawings

Notes * Anything * Ideas

Memories

Doodles

Letters

Numbers
1 2 3

Plans

Thoughts

Dreams   Research   Drawings

Notes * Anything * Ideas

Memories

Plans

Doodles

Thoughts

Letters

Numbers
1 2 3

Dreams

Research

Drawings

Notes * Anything * Ideas

Memories

Plans

Doodles

Thoughts

Letters

Numbers
1 2 3

Dreams Research Drawings

Notes　　*　Anything　*　Ideas

Memories

Doodles

Letters

Numbers
1 2 3

Plans

Thoughts

Dreams　　Research　　Drawings

Notes * Anything * Ideas

Memories

Plans

Doodles

Thoughts

Letters

Numbers
1 2 3

Dreams Research Drawings

Notes * Anything * Ideas

Memories

Plans

Doodles

Thoughts

Letters

Numbers
1 2 3

Dreams

Research

Drawings

Notes * Anything * Ideas

Memories

Doodles

Letters

Numbers
1 2 3

Dreams

Research

Plans

Thoughts

Drawings

Notes   * Anything *   Ideas

Memories

Plans

Doodles

Thoughts

Letters

Numbers
1 2 3

Dreams   Research   Drawings

Notes * Anything * Ideas

Memories

Doodles

Letters

Numbers
1 2 3

Plans

Thoughts

Dreams   Research   Drawings

Notes * Anything * Ideas

Memories

Doodles

Letters

Numbers
1 2 3

Dreams Research Drawings

Plans

Thoughts

Notes * Anything * ☼ *Ideas*

Memories

Plans

Doodles

Thoughts

Letters

Numbers
1 2 3

Dreams

Research

Drawings

Notes * Anything * Ideas

Memories

Plans

Doodles

Thoughts

Letters

Numbers
1 2 3

Dreams Research Drawings

Notes * Anything * Ideas

Memories

Plans

Doodles

Thoughts

Letters

Numbers
1 2 3

Dreams   Research   Drawings

Notes   * Anything *   Ideas

Memories

Plans

Doodles

Thoughts

Letters

Numbers
1 2 3

Dreams   Research   Drawings

Notes * Anything * Ideas

Memories

Plans

Doodles

Letters

Thoughts

Numbers
1 2 3

Dreams   Research   Drawings

Notes * Anything * Ideas

Memories

Plans

Doodles

Thoughts

Letters

Numbers
1 2 3

Dreams Research Drawings

Notes   * Anything * Ideas

Memories

Plans

Doodles

Thoughts

Letters

Numbers
1 2 3

Dreams   Research   Drawings

Notes * Anything * Ideas

Memories

Doodles

Letters

Numbers
1 2 3

Dreams

Research

Plans

Thoughts

Drawings

FLIP TO FUN-SCHOOLING!

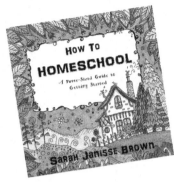

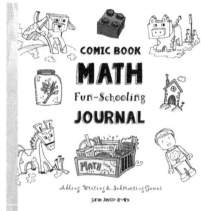

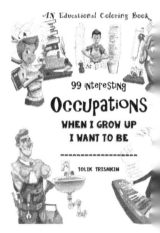

Made in the USA
Columbia, SC
27 July 2020

14733742R00063